Incantations

Poems

Also by Darnell Arnoult:

Galaxie Wagon: Poems (LSU Press 2016)

What Travels With Us: Poems (LSU Press 2005)

Sufficient Grace: A Novel (Atria 2007)

Incantations

Poems

Darnell Arnoult

LAKE DALLAS, TEXAS

Requests for permission to reprint or reuse material from this work
should be sent to:

Permissions
Madville Publishing
PO Box 358
Lake Dallas, TX 75065

Cover Design: Kim Davis
Author Photo: Danny Vaughn

ISBN: 978-1-956440-77-5 paperback
978-1-956440-78-2 ebook
Library of Congress Control Number: 2023947056

For Bryson Joseph Brock

and for Denton Loving

Contents

I.
Knowing

II.
Runners

III.
Barn Star

IV.
Hunt

V.
To Remain Open

VI.
Exist

Imagination, then, must be the flip side of memory,
not so much a calling up as a calling forth.

—Judith Kitchen,
Half in Shade: Family, Photography, and Fate

I.

KNOWING

River breathes your
water's dark body.
Wild premonitions.

SIGHT

Morning bucket of foreknowledge,
a mother's fine victory. Saved
memory is an entry wound

cascading visions wild and murmuring
trembling in the blood. Limbless
night prisms moonlight.

The magic cliff stands high
snake-headed and thickest
right between peace and brotherhood.

Earth frozen and delirious,
drunk enough to be plucked naked
from the war wheel.

Every color mosquito-stomped
and nail-split and vine-locked
and weeds sucking up graveyards.

Bottle fire. Knock down closed yes.
Wide hands hold the scale
and the hill burns where the mother struck.

BENEATH LOVE

Contemptuous problems wait,
somebody's wavering mistake
shoved in the slouching place

behind Hell's snow and kick.
Booze explodes scribbling feet.
Satisfied streets clean demons

backward. Lost. Wrong. Little
else but pockets of problems trailing
sleep. Awful bucktoothed eyes flash

beneath Love's crazy room. Round
and round, come again and again.
Believe in Death. Believe in Love.

Bet cigarettes later. There is no wrong room.
No wrong problem. No wrong place.

EMBODIMENT

Begin half-stupid, mixing the void
with beauty-splintered secrets.
Animal faces bolted eternally
looking for fragmented ghosts
in the stars. Melted into billions
of symbols, once godlike
beasts hammered the curve
of our planet, making a misused
Eden. Reach deep enough
to drift in the blue
shadow of indifferent wings
studded with light years
of dreams and electric poetry.
Breathe the signs.

MORNING

Glory strides up the side of the road, rock strong.
Hear the trees grow enormous, explode with answers.

Its kind current disappears under browed mountains.
It laughs and lumbers over level earth, while ghosts

sigh and watch the quiet valley. Peacefully ferocious,
a spear of creek water cuts and shapes and invents

as it passes, a blade breaking earth and rock.
Glory talks in a hard language. Recognizes ruin.

A condition of everything. She points joy into the void.
Floating in the willow, a bird crows with its entire body.

                              Blind children fix on it and see.

MEMORY

Precious little fingers hold prayer,
believe in a shining heaven of haints
and angels safely heroed in
the arms of a king floating
in a time both golden and safe.

They do not understand our
bodiless history, the serpent,
the fall. Oh, to be the child
holding prayer in my palms.
Oh, that my palms could hold
all the prayers that shadow me.

GAZING OUT

Outlasted windows of lambent horizons
blow open. Wild color and a blizzard of hallelujahs
swoop in. Worn tomorrows wave and twist

and mirror unearthly wishes, knowing.
Ballads shower the shadows and drill down
to a tranquil place where green plumes flash

magic dialogue. Where guitars catch trembling
strings tuned to the music of pure sunrise
crouching in breathless agony. All lost somewhere

among a vast feathering of still rivers of moderation
and striding seas of echo and lightning weather.

II.

RUNNERS

Blind and driven weed
reaches with
abandon—kudzu
hides wild orphans
rust-smothered
escaping all prayers.

HIGH OFFICE

That endless mouth, vast
and immortal, lies transfixed
in fearful prayer. Indicted. Hands
without souls. Arms
without bodies. Dreadful work
to carry away children.
Let there be light.
But the light poems cast
only bounces down the dark hole.
That endless mouth. Lies
crawl and scratch tinted teeth.
The head chokes on weeds
and tangles.
That endless mouth.

LEGEND

Big-armed
hero cradles beasts.
Sings shape into passion.
His cloud-like mask and crown draw ghosts
to life.

VIEW FROM SPACE

Stolen hills, transfigured, watch the unforeseen
swirl of seed and body overbalance. Distend.
Vines trumpet the disappearance of culture's
soul and windshield. Embrace the rebuilt amazement
of home, its concrete ballet. Headlights of ships
cut fear away like a gunshot up terror's highway.

STRUGGLE

Dancing hope squares off with solemn joy.
Blue stones stand massive and absolute as *dead*.

Why must we leap and fly and take and fight
for understanding in such a rock and dust world?

What comes of a static battle of breath and voice
and bearing in a room in a house plagued

by rumbling times and growing reach of men?
Earth fades in tears and heat while we play on,

lying to our children and our planet, and ourselves
the grinding cancer we cannot face or kill or hold off.

LAND FUTURES

Miles of furrows float in contoured loam
as harvest wind screams to undress her common earth.
Splendid farm fields girdle themselves from extinction.
Miles of furrows float in contoured loam,
frail maidens, tragic, vulnerable, dangerous, and clinging,
inexplicably smiling down on impotent desire,
the sleepwalking superhuman fields, incessant and whorish.
Miles of furrows flow in contoured loam
as harvest wind screams to undress her common earth.

REINCARNATION

Plough the broken eggshells,
this broken history mirroring
each floundering human face.

Forgotten birds sail sheer cliffs
of waiting while clouds
of island countries rise enormous

and winged from beneath the sea.
The breast of violence drowns
in a tangle of generations still

treading useless kingdoms.
The enormous feathered breast
of trust reincarnates the world.

Midnight rises, an absolute brace
of dark blue, and star points astonish
and rain shapes of vast beasts

of beauty who mate on the wind.
The ridiculous circle and creak and cry
and dissolve into scuddering cloud lizards.

Glance across the great defeat. Life
can still be found reaching up
from beneath the feet of the dead.

UPHEAVAL

stand in the half-life of change
a country strangely possessed

death's muscle unbuckles at the mouth
and swallows the unbearable

dazzled by words of heaven
enough came between

the shelled and the dazzled
imagine a body without a brain

bodiless ideas that hover and strain
and spread around eaten secrets

dissolve the difference of years
let sweat melt and word sway

stand up to the dog you taste
in your huge and growing tears

INTONE

Sordid implements feign wings—
doctors, drunkards, panhandlers—gambling
fire come holding Lysol labels and broken
warnings. Sleepless bubbles stick to
heroes and intone blowtorch nightlights
wheeling backward into the world.
Fathers amble traffic, drawn down
stilted grill wires. Mothers exhausted,
exhale fire, chairbacks broken, gowns burnt.
Strangers' voices—thieves—crash
like waves. The sound of beehives condemn
power that stiches circles upon circles
of man's sewn and snipped threads.

PROFIT

Mythical bubble explodes and
secrecy comes louder and nearer.
Aluminum brushes thrash the fire.
An angry bear coat moves unnaturally
inside the sharpened diamond.
Scrapes the eye of the sun.
Knits lungs into a mouthpiece
of tumultuous breath and rings
of intimate dissolving rock
until surly aimed dust retreats
and knits and knits more deadly force.

EXODUS CREEK

Human highways rise and fill cloud
roads of sound. Day horses hurtle

quarter moons and daughters dance
with wild turkeys while gamecocks

talk of old pines and gravel. Gold
tracks fill the black mountain. Its weight

settles its own breast, centerless Earth.
Sun rhythms over a howling serpent telling

you rain is long gone and her children,
light as Venus and drunk as owls,

flood judgment. Blind and streaming time
and flowing laurel snag limbs on thorns.

God in the rafters throttles furling breath,
and unwinding roots tell ghosts even night-promised

lust dissolves and speeds mindless and mad
trampling those born of weeds and water.

MOTHY NIGHT

An outlying invasion floats and rises.
Kindness shears miles of freighted light.
Wild decision trains form profound civic
constructs. Secret systems inch sleep
or save or level a sea of pointed expansion.
Dead voices, deep and solar, splinter difference
and hope. Hunger with purpose tends nations.
Hear its craving search. Hear it permeate
the moonlight saunter. Flutter and wing belong
to tumbling time, unstoppable bursting sacks.
Tell me, Grief, is there no strength? No brain?
No roaring fields given over to less than
a raging sea of would-haves?

HAMMERING GENTLY

Fail the shark and blame the gliding
sea. Reach down shipwrecked
beak and feather while unbroken

birds ponder their footsteps
and topsoil walks away, leaving
the endless beach blazing morning.

How these marsh birds still
float on curious blue worlds
gently hammering the sliding waves.

Blazing ghosts, numb and tight-lipped,
dismount their own miracles beside me.
Death glides and dismounts on child-like toes,

her heels shimmering, her infinite feet.
Narrow-thinking pilgrims' curious
miracle stalks rocking planks.

Shall water fail this deep river?
Its undulate sea? This child,
the cloth leaf, shines and changes,

and pelicans nod and nod on this pale
morning, cast also against the thin
black and brittle backs of trees.

LITURGY

Wild worlds of lips burn loud
and boil mean. Furrows shot full of shoulders
double as patient horses in the flaming

curls of unlimited gratitude. Beggars—
strangers—house April's business,
hurt and *hard*. They run God's fences, men

echoing wildfire and dragging a body
bathed in love and dust. Gathered
messages burn across spring pastures.

Turning fields come after spirits free
themselves, and children cry, and women
bawl beyond the crazily smoking limits.

Mean heat loosed. Alive. Doors open
wide. Come close, anyone. Or break
for the woods full of thick-throated fury.

INVENTION

Put on the wheels of bird armor
until the shade of heaven

confronts your breastbone.
Motionless metal mosaics

feature chariots and dog
faces blink in the dazzling

eyepiece of rattling man.
Your weight threatens

my limbs. Cobblestones
curve and crown the silenced

mouth ablaze and shooting
cindery fevers to flower

the strange gaunt hand
and the beam of nailed wood.

III.

BARN STAR

Eight urgent moths pine
for light in the roof rafters.
A mouse climbs the dark.

NO ONE OWNS HIM

Distant heat flutters and reaches
under our infinite nakedness.

Silently uttered breath touches
his chest. Wings groan and break

the tongue's window.
Hands half-full of buried

darkness lift in petition
in another Earth. Mask

his tortured head, break
his unworldly heart. Begin

praying in tongues. Glide back
in words. Frankness and weeping

stir, turn bound beyond possession.
Beyond delight, or words, or sleep.

Beyond heat, or heart, or prayers
with legs. Begin again. Sweat.

Begin again. Begin again.
Begin again. Begin praying.

HERO (OR OUT IN THE WEEDS)

Cast inward toward the primal sacrifice
are the heart of stars and scars of childhood.
Unpack the glittering temple and summon
the bodiless sculptor of skull and wing.
Shoulder the drops of rain and blood.
Wake unshielded revelation standing
in the nettles and thorn bushes.
Thread and brace its perilous force
coiled and flickering. Walk virgin steps.
Bear uncertain fixity without edges,
that shimmering skin of creation.

SALVAGE

Undersides
of blessings rattle.

Provisions hang from
boughs and brambles.

A film of lies attunes
to woolen thoughts.

Wake the heart
of any purpose,

what is painfully
retrieved

from the thicket's
golden crown.

RECLAMATION

Huddled deep-rooted in darkness
a cancer steadily speaks its office.

Hear with your eyes! Death changes
flesh to sparkle, bodies to forest.

Changes. Your song yet to drift
beyond its window, yet to turn

grasping secrets into hovering
voices of light waking the sleeping

source of the unclasped world.
Open your palm and the grave.

Mouth and fingers plant the army
of light trees   yet alive

in that ultimate storied and magical wood
beyond the sun's Easter choir.

THIS TOO IS CREATION

God's uncanny procedure in His hysterical solitude
is to night-bomb the mysterious void. Miles

of system-like threads pull the weighty direction of time. A rock
of light splits and shatters. What electric

silence floats on the eye of that mysterious radio? Rushing
waters cross mountains in human's crusty

sleep. Long-toothed mercy glows in the steel craters
of each face of nothing and something.

HIGHLINE

A river of boxcars drifts down through penny sleep.
Belief's ponderous engine spins and hammers

and stretches. A rockslide monument, a flying
lover threading layers of Earth's crimson breast.

Angels' lanterns shine midair, waking the lives
of the uninspired. The Spirit sings the masterwork

between the rails and the nails and the sky-blinded
faces. A guitar rides in His work-gloved hands.

LOVE FEVER

One dreamer waits on soul things.
Voices pour child-chatter caught

in radio night. Courtly drunkards
disappear, respectful and smiling,

up inadequate staircases. Afternoon
hours worry and twine. Indifference

bears the Earth with pink arms wrongly
turned round four letters, love, still saying

generations and generations. Once
a love fever, it now tinges light and night.

Four letters, home, stiffened and staring, disappear.
Tuned rooms ride pain in the peace

place. Lie six slanted and burning.
The low years by lies fail and rain

ruin in the dreamers' dying. Fingers
helplessly escape inmost change.

Catch straight toward ceiling
a healthy wind. A squirrel existence.

Still, afternoons turn and fade
in waves of caught light.

LIKE ANGELS

Thunderous women without breasts,
whistling beasts of heaven on a mission,
not angels, but islands of fire, strange

and nameless, shouldered with hope,
scratched out of muliebral imagination,
a man's terror, a house of man's time-tired

breath, hiss at the painted king's heart without
legs, without his serpents. Children's lips
attempt a song filled with a rack of haunted

shapes. A bodiless voice speaks of strange ground,
strange times, painted with silvery shadows.
Look how those bronze drums of heavy sweat

swell and float. All in a bowl of ruin. But these
armed, statue-chested heroes, with their might
and drums, beat back a helpless history.

They climb time's tired teeth. Stroke
heaven's worn harp. Shatter the dog-tired armor.
Shine a magical prayer into a humanly ring of years.

IV.

HUNT

Dogs river grassy acres.
Their eyes shine fire.
Heat glides off speckled bodies.
Engine hearts burn,
exploding the night.

WHAT WE KNOW

Tangled songs wait outside the foxhole.
Sweat-tinged prisoners of food and
ghosts dream hooved minds, billowing
beasts, and temple flowers.
A long burn pulses
thinking pillows.
Still, grass and
grave dust
yearn.

PASSING

Perceptive enough, the human gaze licks itself
with the fascination of sorrow.

Line and curve glitter, and still
unearthly arms require neither

bird nor bush. Home holds the slack taste
of changing leaves. A son still intently watches

the cold dust drift earthward. Barns and graves
shift and graze, confident the essence of fields

will hold fixed in harmony beside churches
and bejeweled branches. But love shifts in midair,

itself not bitter or uneasy, forgetting
the heart and the body, requiring no farewell.

MISDIRECTION

long-necked patience rusts

      forms drops of impossible dreams
         on the crowns of the kind and the dead

green-willed sons armed with love

      first wellspring of conjure cry
         long-necked patience rusts

even a place even a stone

      even a fiery briar even
         on the crowns of the kind and the dead

oh dull and heavenly birth

      and the dead unable to inherit
         while long-necked patience rusts

distance delivers   stills all silence

      blood is caught in the wind
         on the crowns of the kind and the dead

the Father and the Son once glazed

      in merciful wood and heavenly pain
         long-necked patience rusts

      on the crowns of the kind and the dead

MALADY

Green shade spirits tremor,
hatch aimless faces,

useless and toothless, falling
under icy repose. Stone cells

settle deeper into clear
wedges of sky and river,

nourishing the most profound place
within a trout's heart.

Overswelling, it roars
and leaps higher in the fire.

Keeps the dogs hunting
stumps of ourselves.

PRAYER

Beneath the sleeping lighthouse
where long-gone midnight
looms like an essential myth

intuition rips past the unborn
body of arcing time. Unchanging,
it struggles sodden and collected,

wrenched from lust-pebbled thighs.
Look for lies concealing a world of light.
Mica sparks and gleams,

inlaid beneath the dust, waiting
among mass intentions to landslide.
Again, it sways and falls silent.

Huge animals breathe, waiting miles
upstream to cross the woods' floor.
To square the dark thicket, their young

wives and children, frail and useless,
bundle up in memories blue and
vague, strange shapes only wandering

the lane of snapping letters. Travel
the sleepy intuition of waiting words.

MOTION

Begin the pursuit of moonlight,
dogs running bridges to sleep,
breath wandering hypnotized through dreams.
Holiness itself dazzling dark seams
of agitation. Come poised for change.

Come poised for touching tongue
to fingers and fingers to wind.
Hold the embers to kill the chill.
Come outside and hear
the outcry of fish and animals.

Shake mistakes and quicken
my rested brain with floating fire foxes
assembling nails and wood into trees.
Pursue moonlight and smile
as night burns the bed.

NIGHT WARS

Awake, you glowing, blazing women
swimming beneath unappeased demands

of these unsleeping wooly worlds
and lifetimes of unreasonable forgiveness.

Glass night's brittle, mythical threshold
surfaces beneath unsleeping dawn

of human folk and their moon strings
strung fleshly across those body guitars.

Steel-fierce, caught in the nylon wound of human waiting,
unappeased eyes drown in a pool of fierce clucking blood,

patting savagery and doom,
battling terminal temperate touching.

Light surviving windows and cold
abandoned-child places, lie

unsleeping, carrying battles
          on shoulders, believe pillows are terminal—

          dreams weighing anything but light.
How many precious breathing curves

          sealed in my own forgivelessness would it
          take to hover and float? Enough

          to rise like a thousand streaming moons?
Enough to breathe in the fishy light?

EVOLUTION SONNET

Cracked cocktail of the newly risen
unknowable, creek dirt under
the table, impression of love
open-throated and drawn down
with my own cold edge of night.
Ragged wings of the first morning
tongues fluttered under water.
Hooves darkened the bank enough
to lift sunlight into long weightless
autumn. Knee to ground. Earth
to wing. Pink-mouthed leaves.
But not before knowing the ledge
and gap, stoop and scream,
crest and pit. Love evolved and holding.

V.

TO REMAIN OPEN

Love allotted hurtles
like raging stars to some
tough and poetic parting.

PICKUP

Grinning altar of twenty years warbling
variations of thriving light.
Hear that powdery sound of ashes.
Hear that crackling sound of unfired absolution.

Hear the warbling neighbors and grinning
children, nervous and amiable, a clashing
band of flames dancing at the threshold.
Invalid tongues split and spit out reason.

The thing is, deep gentle reason shows
nothing called meaning. Dying levels
out. Still, imagine a hummingbird.
Those two wings curving a thousand

breathless cymbals. Imagine tongues split
and hear lungs ring the dying dance.
Sock-footed nothing. Dark matter.
Breathe in the traveling music.

WIDOWHOOD

Peer passed vibrant stalks of rain. Think of his absent face
now uncaught by earth, light among stars. The man

is now stardust. His voice like the riddle of dreams.
Whoever unfailingly loves a cowboy, truly loves him,

steps closer, hand-to-hand and head-to-head, the connection
like home, until falling is the only tangible move.

It waits forward unobstructed amongst the stringy sawgrass
somewhere in the dead of winter, somewhere past the speed of light.

SORROW

slowly night pieces like rain
floats fringed across killing needles

tingling dosage   brothers of the million
dead and dying sleepwalk roads ready for fish

swimming pine logs and dusty creatures—
long curled stone against dreamed current

blood and wind   roads unsplit   and I am
the moon-licked foot   lost   dry   surprised

at what it leaves
I have been flagged (save me)

fallen underneath the hill-hacked quivering
stump   held   giving dry quiver of something

back from the momentarily dreamed
problem   arm-shot   dusty   rising deadly

ground after ground after new ground
all cut deep

STORM

The long grasses spelling wind
stubbornly square growing clouds.
Green-lidded seasons past
increase wonders, ancient veins

stubbornly square and growing clouds.
Catch age and contrary flame.
Increase wonders, ancient veins,
sighing splinters and birds,

catching age and contrary flame,
beat air away and years speak.
Sighing splinters and birds
and tremoring harbors

beat air away and years speak.
My grass blades single-minded
and tremoring harbors
through open roads and squall.

My grass blades, single-minded
green-lidded season, pass
through open roads and squall,
long grasses spelling wind.

REBIRTH

a clownish moon winces to be born upward and sideways
breath of stone   circling smoke   waits midair for itself
and touches coronas of scrolling glass halos

silent bedsheets muddied and falling
the sun like upward curtains of flame
tears tangle and crack in the whiteness

perpetual feathers shout the color of the heart
consuming light glows anew and stars hold tight
shine together a brace of searing ointments

dazed eyes walk the billowing latitudes
of bathing years   crisscrossed tongues scream
love and cool water and this blazing bed

ENGINE

Ghosts, like thoughts, pound
out new wings in a shaking hole.
Their crackling gyros linger.

With huge and brilliant heads,
angels sweep down an island of light
and rattle the delicious milky moon.

Watch how we widows hold our hellish turn
and clear the heat of a slaughtered
and emptied heart. Bolts of invisible sorrow

swish and circle—hot and crackling—
gathering the thousands of widows,
banged and busted by death's auto-pilot.

Hell's earphone whispers the scope
of the ghosts' brilliant wings. Rest.
Cool your split spirit, they say.

We drift right beneath you.
Life is a ship running the sword
of God's watch and the sucking speed

of all else bouncing between stars
and the devilish ground. Until some one thing
finally undoes the hatch of hours.

REBIRTH II

Somewhere wolves listen, dead to the eye.
Hear the immortal farm boy rise
to save the west and wake reason.

Now hear the beast groan and die.
Listen for failing hellishness.
I saw the great hillside reborn

in kindness and love. Tell the world
to look for pastures filled with dewy grass.
The wind stirs the field and whirls the Earth

saying remember the terrible
and the great. Remember the soft
wild truth of the mother's love hound.

NEW LIFE

First roped to its surrounding sea,
a child comes out naked and unknown,
swimming to the light and an immortal
piece of shining understanding.
Some strange idling fever of a thought.
Foreign to voice and chattering teeth,
it howls up a strange war garden
of cobbles and blue flowers and dangerous
dogs. A long body of yesterdays—tabled,
tattered, and dying—drops deep into walls
of time and sets into wordless night.

FLOOD

Stuck in passion's boat, a meaningless maelstrom snakes
its summons. Blazing impure and huge, it reaches

unappeasable from sea to mountain, its messageless weight
signifying authority's dim mark. Then frozen winter light

sheds back clouds, and triumph of mind and heart surprises
with its camphoric bones and unopposed sky. Land and lake

flash their fine banner of balance as the river stretches out
like a bolt of cloth unfurled and unhindered. An oar flashes

its treading edge and the stream dreams of a bronze hull,
its curved skin pursuing abandoned direction and embodied worth.

VI.

EXIST

Music is light.
Light is music.
Wellspring's eye.
Look up.

ARCHITECTURE

Mathematics of light and reflection—
moon sponging sun's blinding plume,

shamelessly placing it in moon's gullied
stone womb. Scripture's Spirit does not

doom as reprisal, murder lockjawed.
Orbiting Genesis is the soft, seething body

of a lover, pouring into soul after soul
a solar intellect, scripting and conceiving,

shameless. Its candlesticks are dreams.
Its sex longed for eclipses of whatever

passes for the river of flowing stars in nature's
cosmic brain and our own clouded ideas.

IMMORTALITY

Lies, crest your limits and gleam as fallen
figures. Face the gravity of shucked failings.

Bodiless daybreak, float down the gullies
of dreams shallow as skylight.

Rise and carry every fallen thing into the grave.
Choose to tremble and stretch and walk forward.

LOOK UP

Strangely free, clouds invent
animals on currents of wind,

then slowly recontain young
spirits, creature after creature,

drifting to be reborn in a river
of whiteness, hunting new bodies,

new stories. The sun burns their
ghosts invisible. I stand across

the pasture, rooted in bright flame,
my heart and head keener for climbing

out of this frail creature, myself,
in cadence with the long-hidden

childhood and playground
without earth or body.

VOICE LESSONS

The song is a slave to breath's wave,
shedding its frail pools, pressing ripples
outward, sideways, then turning inward.
Miserly as moonlight shadowing ruins,
body rhythms work toward the sea.
Or is the breath enslaved by the song?

ASSAULT

Ripping landslide of words—
dust's concealing flash

wrenches down across sodden lust.
Humans saddled and reaching,

reaching, as in sleep. An explosion
of utter midnight and struggle stands,

its maniacal afterthought looking
across the beast's darkened world.

But see memories of long-dead essentials
gleam above the dust, stride

upstream, huge and light,
into the frail world. We scramble

in strange times for one
half-breath

of joy lying
dazed and waiting.

INVENTION II

Almighty inflection
flowers, a miracle,
essential luck
meant to shuttle

the coin of rebirth,
split lightning, choke
blind trees, forever
glance after grass
and angels.

PURPOSE OF ART

Graffiti trembles encouragement.
Saturday city ceremony.
A temple cradling clarity.

Morning's silent amazement.
Night's loose-winged
stammer and dream.

Swarms the centerline.
Voices in all directions
shimmer floods of possibility.

DAYLIGHT

Withdrawing
moonlight bends the world toward a resurrection

of birds.
Sun and song calling other tongues to cry away

the shadows.
Fish pack the glassy river as it curves and hears an engine

louder and
righter than any long-haul spiral of mankind's building or striking.

RAPTURE

Footsteps echo survival in the endangered dusk.
The chosen tingle as squalls blast upward

through open time. Watch in the lamp's wake.
In the lyric bleating and drumming, creatures

linger, completely themselves, hearts fathomless
and flickering. Huddled. Alive. Like waifs

at the doorstep. Astounded at the weird
hand we've come to hold.

WORK

Moonlight freely wants its glory,
holy howling eyes singing
heaven's blues. Heaped-up songs
break thrones. Understand sound.
Hidden glory lightly consumes
the double-dog coming. Ankles creek
weighted tears. All mouths touch
my own. An original voice masters its living
tongue. Its giving tongue. Its burning tongue.
Walk it home. Believe in the tree,
in the owl, in the light. Believe and move
from the crouching dark. Cross
grief and master fierce wanting. Walk
your own soul's endless entrance.

Acknowledgments

Acknowledgment and thanks to the editors of the following publications in which some of these poems first appeared, some in slightly different form.

Appalachian Places: Stories from the Highlands: "Daylight" and "Work"
Crossing the Rift: North Carolina Poets on 9/11 and Its Aftermath: "Assault" (Press 53, 2021)
Cutleaf: "Invention," "Passing," "Pickup," "Reclamation," and "Widowhood"
Troublesome Rising: A Thousand-Year Flood in Eastern Kentucky: "Knowing" and "This Too Is Creation" (Fireside Industries, University Press of Kentucky, 2024)

Thank you, Linda Parsons, Kim Davis, and all those associated with Madville Publishing, who made this book possible. Also thank you, among others, Denton Loving, Aaron Smith, and Jesse Graves, who encouraged me early on with these poems; Iris Tillman Hill for excellent advice; Sue Dunlap, Connie Green, Vicki Brumback, Carole Stice, Carol Grametbauer, the late Joyce McDonald, and all the members of Chapbook and Novel Workshop at Learning Events; Harry and Sue Richardson Orr; my wonderful book club—Patti Meredith, Lynn Moss Sanders, Jo Garrison, Van Garrison, Ann Thomas, Barbara Lucky, Diana Young-Paiva, Grace Evans; Lee Smith, Tom Ranking, Jill McCorkle, Judy Goldman, Abigail Dewitt, Michael Chitwood, Joseph Bathanti, Melissa Helton, Lynn York, Pamela Duncan, Virginia Boyd, Calvin Hall, Lauren Walter, Sonja Livingston, Alan Holmes, Lucinda MacKethan, Jim Minick, Georgann Eubanks, and Donna Campbell and all the Table Rock Writers Workshop gang; Dana Wildsmith, Jane Hicks, Lisa Parker, Belinda Smith, Robert Gipe, Shawna Kay Rodenberg, Wendy Dinwiddie, Noah Avarez, Katlin Brock, Susan Gregg Gilmore, Ruth Petty Jones, Tony Maxwell, and Joe Wofenbarger; all my wonderful students (old and young); and my former colleagues at Lincoln Memorial University. Most of all, thank you to my family. None of my work would be possible without their encouragement and support—particularly Beth and Alex MacKethan and Xander; Chad and Jody Stone and Virginia; Vivian; Emerson, my running and reading partner; Bryson Brock; and, most particularly, my late husband and cowboy, William Brock. My love overflows.

About the Author

Darnell Arnoult is the author of the poetry collections *Galaxie Wagon* and *What Travels With Us* (LSU Press) and the novel *Sufficient Grace* (Simon & Schuster), with shorter works in literary journals and anthologies. She has received the Weatherford Award, SIBA Poetry Book of the Year Award, the Thomas and Lillie D. Chaffin Award, and the Mary Frances Hobson Medal for Arts and Letters and was nominated for a Pushcart Prize. For 10 years she was writer-in-residence at Lincoln Memorial University, where she directed the Mountain Heritage Literary Festival, the Appalachian Young Writers Workshop, and summer writing workshops and retreats through Arts in the Gap. She was a founding editor of *drafthorse: a literary journal of work and no work*. Originally from Henry County, Virginia, Arnoult now lives with family in Mebane, North Carolina, where she teaches private writing workshops and is a faculty member of Table Rock Writers Workshop and John C. Campbell Folk School.

Learn more at www.darnellarnoult.net.

Printed in the USA
CPSIA information can be obtained
at www.ICGtesting.com
LVHW020738080324
773863LV00005B/106